Psychological Awareness
of a **Nature Photographer**

Tom Spencer

Thank you to:

Alison Hardie

Author's Notes

Alone in nature I found myself. My soul has grown and the camera tells the story.

Contents:

Chapter 1

The Joys of Nature Photography

Nature photography is, at least in my experience, the least stressful form of photography. It is a natural art form that gives a sense of belonging, freedom, and promotes self awareness on many levels, including both artistically and spiritually. From an artistic point of view, joy often comes from the ability to successfully replicate the image we are seeing and the feelings we experience at that moment. We may get added satisfaction from making the scene look even better using camera techniques and tricks. Knowing we have accomplished this and have created an image that others are likely to enjoy pushes us to make the next image have an even greater impact on the viewer, each and every time. Spiritually, nature photography connects us with something within ourselves we did not even know we were disconnected from. This aspect is harder to explain and may be something you can only understand once you allow yourself to become aware of it.

Another joy of the hobby comes from sharing our images. This is much easier when we can transfer files to anyone using the internet. The practice of submitting portfolios or CDs through the mail is becoming less popular while file hosting services such as DropBox are making file sharing easy. Social media today is a great motivator in the pursuit of fine-tuning our creative skills in nature photography, as peers encourage us by "liking" and sharing our work. Positive feedback feeds our motivation. Having our images is extremely satisfying for most. Another source of satisfaction is the personal goal of exceeding our own standards.Every time we photograph a subject and exceed our own expectations, we set the bar higher for what we consider acceptable standards. This ladder of goal setting we climb may never end but with every new step it feeds our hunger to work at a higher level.

For me, nature photography is not so much about the sharing of photos that I love, as it is more personal than that. An important part of the experience involves putting in the effort and going home with high quality nature photos I can be proud of, the chase of a good photo, and playing cat and mouse with luck. The longer I spend in the backwoods of my town, the more effort I feel went into my photo adventure that day, even if it means sitting in the same spot for two hours waiting for something to happen. Another part for me, and for many other nature photographers, is simply the love of being outdoors in the first place, and the photography is simply a bonus. This is an oasis we can escape to after work, school, or whatever your schedule has you a prisoner to. It is filled with colour, smells, feelings and a personal connection to something bigger than can be explained. The best poetry only describes a small part of this experience, and our photography reminds us of what we see in it and in ourselves. There is a lure to the forest for the nature photographer, as if some of us are wilder than others.

For some that I have met, this attraction is all about the animals. The hunt is thrilling and the photo at the end is the paramount factor. Whether there is much of a hunt or not, the photo is the trophy, the bragging rights and the more exotic the wildlife, the bigger and brighter the trophy. Whether you have a personal checklist or you just like to compare fictitious trophies with your peers, the itch that keeps you hunting for the next animal on your checklist is the same for the bird photographer, landscape photographer or any other nature photographer. For this reason, we should pat each other on the back, not scratch.

There is a type of nature photographer that we tend to cross paths with in the photography community whom I like to call "the fisherman". This is the type of person that enjoys photography but with little to no concern about the technical aspect of the equipment. This is someone who is simply out looking for opportunities while enjoying the time spent outdoors. Any image captured is a good catch for the fisherman, whether it is big or small, sharp or blurry. If a fisherman invites you out to take photos, it is important and highly recommended that you do not show off your tackle box. Go out, relax, enjoy the time spent and keep a chapter in your book of all the things the fisherman has taught you.

Ask yourself what it is that you get out of nature photography. Is it the photography or is it nature? Maybe it is a combination of both or maybe it is something deeper. Whatever it is, it is up to you to find out what keeps you going. This book will help you discover yourself, and it is yourself that will then take you where you need to go.

Chapter 2

Technology vs Creativity

There is an endless amount of creativity that can be applied to photography. However, your ability to express yourself the way you want may be limited by the capabilities of your equipment. In my experience, I have found that when I thought I had outgrown my camera, I was still able to use it to its full capability and express myself the way I wanted. Upgrading the equipment was not as vital as I had thought. Try to recognize that you may not need to replace your equipment and that wanting to and needing to are different things.

I would almost go as far as to recommend using older

equipment and to limit your capabilities when taking pictures. This will challenge your ability to achieve what you want and encourage creative ways of thinking. Getting your hands on a film camera can have many benefits for the digital shooter. You will know when it is time for an upgrade and when you do so, be sure to explore all the new abilities you have. Staying with older equipment for too long can also slow your growth, so be aware of this issue as well.

Not being able to upgrade your equipment as soon as you would like might seem like a handicap, but remember, you got this far with what you have so do not dwell on it too much. When you make the decision to upgrade, take comfort in the fact that it is only a matter of time and enjoy taking photos until then.

Advancements in post-processing seem to come quicker than anything else in the world of photography. Try to keep up to date with the latest editing software and do not be afraid to experiment out of your comfort zone with the alterations to your images. In the day and age of digital photography, editing is just the icing on the cake.

Chapter 3

Your Attitude and Your Photos

Your attitude will affect your photos, just as it affects all your day-to-day actions. It is important that you understand how you are being affected. Understanding how the two are connected is the first step to correcting your attitude. For example, a negative attitude affects the outcome of the entire photo trip. If a person has a negative attitude while seeking out wildlife and having little to no success, a negative attitude will elicit a sense of hopelessness for that location, the wildlife, and the tactics used to seek out opportunities. A positive attitude will leave the photographer with a "better luck next time" feeling, and allow them to be able to learn from their mistakes, rather than giving up due to negativity. Understanding and recognizing how your attitude can affect you is an important step in becoming successful. Once the camera becomes a part of you, understanding yourself and being aware of the influences that make you behave the way you do is important. Learn to recognize your moods and how they may be affecting you. Take control of your moods and understand that your mind is a filter. When events happen to you in your life, your mind filters those experiences in two different ways, either positive or negative. If your mind deems a situation or event as a positive experience it will alter your mood in a positive way. Being in a positive mood of course will clear the road for positive outcomes for yourself. It is easier to get through your day when you are in a positive mood. The opposite can be said for filtering negative experiences. A negative experience will most likely alter your mood in a negative way. The problem is, it is difficult to make positive outcomes for yourself when you are in a bad mood. All of this of course you already realize because we all live and experience this on a daily basis. Now you are likely thinking, get to the point! This is the power that you possess. You may not have realized it, but your mind has the ability to filter negative experiences in a positive way to create positive outcomes in your life. It will take some practice to develop this way of thinking. This works as an advantage to an artist. The ability to control your attitude will only work in your favour. Learn to see the positive and you will discover much about yourself. When you have a clear self-image and self-understanding you will be unable to fail.

Common Attitudes Towards Photography

Confidence can be the difference between taking the shot or not. For example, you have to allow a certain level of confidence to drive you in order to pursue a photo opportunity that may be challenging to capture. If your subject is at a distance, whether it be flora or fauna, it is worth taking the time to get up close. Having the confidence to know you can get a great shot if you get yourself within range will drive you to target that subject. If your efforts fail you will be no further back; just take note of any mistakes you made and continue. Your self-confidence will increase as your photography improves. Your achievements and new goals will allow you to build confidence as they are reached. Be aware of any negative thoughts that can hinder your confidence.

Competition should never play a part in nature photography. I personally have always looked at nature photography as a solo adventure. Like many others, I am self-taught and believe that, although it is a slower progression it requires harder lessons to be learned. Other than the company of my dogs, I feel that having that personal space in the woods alone is critical for me to concentrate on finding creative ways to capture little pieces of my surroundings.

Like everything, there is a social side that you can choose to be a part of that has great benefits and also great disadvantages. The obvious benefits are having others to learn from, and having others constructively critique your work, and provide motivation and inspiration. The list goes on and I am sure you have had some benefits from a social group by now. You do have to take some caution, as every time you have a group of people sharing an interest, politics will eventually come into play. It is important to be aware that social politics are distractions that can keep you from growing as a photographer. These man-made issues are irrelevant to why you love photography and where you are going on your journey as an artist. Compete with yourself, not others, and let others compete with you.

Mood vs Attitude

Your mood is a feeling at a particular time. Events can alter your mood in both a negative and positive way. We have many moods and we all go experience them. Controlling a mood can be difficult as it is human nature to have different moods arise from different situations. Your mood will affect your photography in different ways, as when you recognize the mood you are in you have a choice to either fight it or allow it to affect your photography. Neither decision is the wrong decision; the point is that you have the psychological strength to recognize that your mood is affecting the outcome of your photos. Attitude, on the other hand, is how we perceive a situation. We can change the way we think about the situation that presents itself, even if our mood is getting in the way. For example, you may be out taking pictures with little success and to make things worse it starts raining and you realize you are five miles away from your vehicle. This may put you in a bad mood, but you can choose what attitude you take towards the situation. New opportunities present themselves in the rain and give you a second chance at leaving with quality photographs you did not anticipate and can be proud of. The way you see things will change the things you see.

Photography, especially nature photography, has many chapters. To understand all of them, you first need to understand yourself. In the beginning, understand what you want out of photography, and do not rush anything. After some time, appreciate what you have accomplished, what challenges you have gone through to get to where you are and how well you are doing now. After you feel like you have run a marathon, look back and take note of each mile because it is just starting.

Chapter 4

Personal Emotional Challenges

One of the hardest challenges for the occasional nature photographer is something you would assume is out of your control: finding time to go shoot. Days are short, we have busy schedules and we are often left with no time or not enough time to take pictures, something I regularly struggle with. In my experience, finding time to shoot was the one non-mental barrier that would delay my hobby and slow my rate of improvement. Over the years, as I let a lack of hours in the day set back my goals again and again, I realized that finding time to pursue your passion is the most challenging mental barrier you have to face. I say this because to have time to squeeze photography into your busy day, you have to make time. We do not "find it" at all, as we need to put time aside and throw out the wasted time being used on inconsequential activities that contribute nothing to our happiness. Time is made for the people and activities you love. I am not suggesting better time management, although this is an option; I am suggesting that less time be wasted. You have the discipline to make time for photography, it is a matter of having conscious awareness that you can do this. Do more of what you love.

Relationships- Without going into detail, I, like many of you, have fallen victim to a hopeful yet impractical relationship. This experience left me stunned in a hypnotic way that, for a while, made me unaware of how much I had been affected. I became lethargic in my shooting, photographing meaningless subjects in a careless, inattentive way as if my photography was on autopilot. My head and heart were somewhere else and they are the two crucial components that make up a photographer. Over time, I was able concentrate on the picture more and more and that picture reminded me of her less and less. The same will happen to you if you can relate to this chapter. It is true, I think, that time heals all wounds.

Death- Dealing with death is not easy, and in my case, it was the death of my furry friend, my husky/collie mix named "Bogart". This was the most difficult emotional challenge I have had to face yet, and the only one that completely shut down my photography. In the beginning, I would practice nature photography while I walked my dogs and over time my skills grew, which led to spending more time focusing on the picture. The dogs (Gabby and Bogart) of course wanted to get a move on. My solution was to walk the dogs, bring them home and then go back with the camera. This strategy did not last long before I was back at it with the dogs and the camera. Without knowing it, the dogs became my photography partners and a lot of the time my subjects as well. Gabby, who was Bogart's mom, died first and it was very sad. I still had Bogart, however, and we were particularly close, whereas Gabby had a more independent spirit. My photography continued and so did our walks. Bogart seemed fine despite losing his mother, but one year after Gabby's passing, Bogart got sick with cancer. This left my family with the hard task of deciding when to put him down before he suffered too much, but also trying not to rob him of life. My photos were only of him when he was sick and when he died my photography stopped completely.

This book was already in its rough copy stages during Bogart's fight and so I knew I would be dealing with emotions that would affect my photography. I think I made a conscious choice to not take pictures at the time, and to give my heart time to heal so my mind could focus on the hobby I love so much. Almost one year later as I write this, I still do not enjoy our old trail as much as I used to. Some things in life affect us deeply, and with nature photography being such a personal, intimate art it is no wonder the craft will also be affected. These events shape us, make us stronger, and give our art direction. You become who you are through the emotional challenges life gives us, and your artistic eye will reflect this in your photographs.

Stress- Being stressed presents a handful of challenges for the nature photographer, the greatest challenge being that it takes you out of the moment. Stress keeps thoughts on the past or the foreseeable future. You are trying to come up with solutions to the cause of the stress, and will likely be talking to yourself out loud. To bring yourself back, you first need the psychological awareness to acknowledge that you are in the wrong state of mind. You may realize this when you are out on your walk, whether you have a camera or not to help with the stress. Once you bring yourself back mentally, stop in your tracks and breath deep. Next, close your eyes and listen to nature, it is all right if you can hear the highway or trains in the distance. Now, look through your viewfinder and compose the closest subject to you; whether you press the shutter or not is up to you. Now, if you continue on your walk you will feel as if you just hit your internal restart button. Of course, if something is still bothering you, that is fine, as you are human. The point is, you just demonstrated the power to change your state of mind, and you will find this feeling of having control gratifying.

Changing seasons- A very real mental problem for some is the winter blues. Less sunlight, often a change in diet, and going outside less are just a few of the possible issues that result in the winter blues. Winter can be a struggle, so having the task of being creative in your hobby during grey times does not help. My only advice on this issue that I personally struggle with every year is to face it head on as a challenge. Look at it as a long-distance race. Expect it to be long, and do not worry about the end; just take it a bit at a time. Winter offers opportunities that are not available other times of the year and this can be a positive thing. Still, I will admit that the only definite cure is spring.

Adrenaline- I recently experienced an adrenaline rush during a trip photographing coyotes that challenged my ability to focus on the task at hand. A combination of their close proximity to us, the size of the animals and the realization of a perfect opportunity left me shaking with adrenaline. I did not realize it during the moment, but after reviewing the photos I was stunned to find most of them blurry. How could this be? I thought that I had used a shutter speed more than adequate for the conditions. My photography partner later told me he heard me gasping for air as if I was holding my breath the whole time. I then realized in the excitement that I seemingly had no control, and this affected my photos a great deal. All I can do now is laugh, and try and have more control over myself next time an exciting opportunity arises. Breathe, stay calm, realize the mental challenge and steady your hands.

Creative Rut- You may think you are in a bit of a creative rut, but are you really? Thinking back to my earlier years as a photographer, I believe I have gone through four major photography "ruts". Fast forward through the miracle of time and now I can tell you what really happened, and is likely happening to you. Think of your photographic journey as a ladder and every time you take a step the step behind you falls off. There is no going down, only up. You are taking pictures and you will get a very special shot that to you is like skipping a step up the ladder to perfection, and two steps behind you fall off. What I am trying to say is that you got a shot so great that your standards reached a new level! The photos you were taking before no longer satisfy this new standard for photography, yet we continue to photograph many shots that would fall off the standards ladder. Until you get another shot as visually eye-popping and continuously do so, we are left behind in a creative rut, stuck in the middle, dying to move up. We all go through this, and the more photographs you take and the less hope you lose, the faster you will climb and reach the level where you want to be. Just keep going!

What I want you to take away from this chapter is that, as humans, we have the ability to control our state of mind. Realize the emotional challenge and stand up to face it. Your thoughts control your mood and your thoughts are controlled by you. Gain control and control your life. Do not let negative thoughts alter your mood. Realizing the emotional challenge you are facing is the first step to correcting it so you can achieve a positive outcome. The ability to have positive thoughts after a negative situation makes you very powerful. From there, you can bring your mood back to a calm state and do less damage to your creativity.

Chapter 5

Self-Healing

Photography as a de-stressor. The therapeutic side of nature photography.

You may be a professional or specialist, customer care agent or tradesman during the week. On the weekend, however, you are an artistic composer, in a therapeutic environment, focused yet relaxed. You are a nature photographer.

  Photography has always been my escape. When emotions and life's challenges are thrown at me, I have always considered nature photography a form of free therapy. The hobby to me was always a de-stressor, but when I really needed it, I just had to dig a little deeper and be more aware of myself. The nature aspect of course is a huge part of the healing process when you need it, but I believe that the camera plays a large role as well. You may not even be taking pictures depending on how you are feeling that day but knowing you can and that the tool is with you as you go for a walk or drive is a nice feeling. I bet you know what I am talking about. Ultimately it is you, and your psychological awareness as a photographer that cleans the toxins from your mind. Nature, and the camera are just the tools we use to concentrate our creative energy into something we can see. The therapeutic side of nature photography for me is the creative process of taking the images, enjoying solitude, and the reward of a good shot. It may be different for you, but whatever your reasons are, embrace them.

We all know that when we are upset over something, the hard part is being aware of how it is affecting you and the way you are looking at things. As much as you would like to storm around and talk to yourself, replaying conversations that went wrong and making them right in the bush while you are taking pictures, just stop for a second and breath. Once you recognize your emotions you now have options. You can control them and focus on your photography, which is easier said than done, or sit, relax and let your emotions become calm. Just like we get ourselves worked up, we also have the ability to calm ourselves down. One is obviously harder than the other, but the point is that you are aware of it because so many people tend to forget. Being aware of the emotional state you are in is the first step to controlling it.

Before you walk down a trail, a good exercise to use to clear your mind is to stop, close your eyes and breath deep through your nose, exhale slowly out your mouth and repeat this three times. Then, open your eyes and begin your photo session. Try this and you will notice a calming feeling come over you.

I believe that all the time I spent alone in the woods taking pictures over the years has given me a clear vision of who I am. Not just as a photographer but as a person. The time spent indulging in my thoughts has allowed me to come to know my outlook on everything. This feeling of self-understanding relieves me of fear in different aspects of my life: past, present and future.

Chapter 6

Remembering Where You Started

How we change

If you look at your past work, your best work, you will see how much you have changed as a photographer. All these changes we go through are mental. Of course, some equipment changes along the way will be made, but the biggest change happens internally. Over the years, or even months, your standards have changed in terms of what "makes the cut". But what is it that transformed these standards? I can only speak for myself on this, but for me I believe the biggest change was discovering myself. With all the hours and kilometres we put behind us when taking pictures, a lot of thinking and self-discovering is going on, even when we do not know it. I discovered self-worth through seeing the value in what I was doing. This has not only been valuable to my happiness, but to others that may enjoy my work. This assessment of my own value on this planet came early, as I felt I was meeting high standards in my photography at the time. I accepted my role as a nature photographer and subconsciously decided to dedicate the rest of my life to this hobby. I feel as if the ingredients that make up my soul and make up who I am as a person have come to light because of this hobby.

Do I owe this hobby something for giving me a sense of belonging? Or do I owe something to myself for digging deep and discovering that I am now what I set out to be as a person and as an artist. Identify the changes you have gone through over the years, keep track of your growth and it will guide you into the future.

Sometimes you can be in an area long enough to feel like you have photographed every possible subject twice. The reality is that your favourite trail is always providing you with new possibilities, especially as the seasons change. The good photos become harder to recognize as we get bored with an area.

We can only photograph something for the first time once, so too much repetition can leave us feeling disinterested. If it is necessary, take a break from that location for a while or perhaps blaze a new trail off of an old one you are familiar with. This helps to keep things fresh, and your eyes will quickly target new subjects to photograph.

Looking back at old photographs is a powerful motivator. Some photos more than others are connected to strong emotions, all for our own reasons. Looking back five years ago at a fox photo, my mind floods with memories and my heart is flooded with old emotions. How far I drove to get there, where I stopped for food that day, who I was with and how I felt when we came across the fox den. It all hits you at the same time and I want to feel that again. I want to go back and do it all the exact same way or better yet, go back in time for one more ride, but I know I can not. What I can do though, is get out and start a new adventure, find new places and new subjects and in five years from now I will look back and see how far I have come and be inspired by my old photo adventures once again.

Chapter 7

Moving Forward

What does the future hold for me as a photographer? How far do I want to take this adventure? These are questions I am sure you have asked yourself. For some of my friends in the industry, some common questions they ask themselves are "Am I too old to pursue this in the way I want?" "Do I have enough time?" and "What am I really trying to get out of this?" These are all questions I have been asked and at a time have asked myself. The answer to these questions will change as time goes on because as we progress our goals change and we look at photography differently.

We all have more than one image of ourselves. One image is a reflection of what we see in ourselves now, while another is where we want to be or where we wanted to be by now. Keep your goals in sight and your image of yourself will quickly become your reflection. Your character is strengthened by the countless hours spent pursuing the subjects you love, sometimes in conditions that challenge even the toughest person, hours spent alone with your thoughts waiting for the perfect light or wildlife to pass by. This tenacity gives us better stamina for future ambitions, which is something we can use in our everyday lives.

My advice for moving forward would be to keep your expectations as a nature photographer reasonable and let the art teach you and guide you on a natural path to success. We all have a different idea of what we consider success, yet I know the day will come for everyone when you realize that you are where you want to be as a photographer right now. Continue to let nature photography be a healer. When your vision is blurred and you are struggling to get past obstacles in life, the benefits of nature photography will become clear.

Chapter 8

What We Leave Behind

Since I am still here it is hard to say what I will leave behind. The obvious is shoe boxes full of nature images. Or full hard drives of raw and jpg files. I hope to leave behind something more valuable than that. I hope and believe that someone will see the value in the photographs and look at them in a way that allows them to see my story and understand the character that pushed the shutter that day. As photographers, we are blessed to leave behind more of ourselves than others are able to. However, it is still sad that the memories, the moments leading up the click of the shutter and the satisfaction of hearing the sound will remain only with me.

This, perhaps, is but a small price to pay for the value of what we are leaving behind.

This chapter is like a black and white image. We can picture it in colour but unless we were there, we will never exactly know the true image.

Be sure to take the care to save your work in ways that are archival. We are living in a time of files, hard drives, and online file storage. Paper copies stored in a safe place still seem to be the saving grace when luck runs out.

In the present, continue to shoot for you. You are your worst critic and yet your biggest fan. There is no one you should be trying to impress more. Keep your motivations personal and allow yourself to grow with the hobby. What you leave behind will be a reflection of your soul and there is nothing better on this Earth you can possibly share than that.

www.ingramcontent.com/pod-product-compliance
Lightning Source LLC
Chambersburg PA
CBHW081148170526
45158CB00009BA/2764